EMISSARY

Alex Chornyj

ISBN: 978-93-6354-267-9

First Edition: 2025
Rs. 200/-

Cyberwit.net
HIG 45 Kaushambi Kunj, Kalindipuram
Allahabad - 211011 (U.P.) India
http://www.cyberwit.net
Tel: +(91) 9415091004
E-mail: info@cyberwit.net

Printed at Repro India Limited.

Dedicated to my darling daughter Luna

Contents

Emissary

Some time ago
You were called by nature
To do an act of kindness
Out of the goodness,
Of your caring heart
To go to a forest
Not in your neck of the woods
With the Sequoias,
In California
You went unknowing
Exactly what it was
You were supposed to do.
When you got there
A change came over
The reason was as clear
As the stars shining at night.
You were to attend
Within a circle of trees
When you reached your destination
A beacon would,
Then reveal itself
As you entered inside
You knew this was sacred ground
Your presence was felt,
By those who brought you forth
As you were once one of them
So went about
A healing ceremony.
So set your hands

Down into the earth
You as the conduit
Rejuvenated a land.
When this channeling
Came to an end
You heard a melody
Coming from a golden dragonfly.
He who hovered
For what seemed like an eternity
Was your father as an emissary
Thanking you for the light you had shared.

Carving-Caring Current

You go where others have not
So step with purpose
Hide behind nothing
Call this as you see it.
Are a free spirit
Bound only by conscience
You're of an old soul
From these depths come wisdom.
So when you speak
Others tend to listen
With a hunger
In a search for knowledge.
As you have been around
The seven continents
The five oceans
And dimensions in between.
You have a way
Puts you on the map
For all the right reasons
Signs lead from all directions.
To find your doorstep
Not by coincidence
But manifestation
To hear of your words.
As each syllable
Has its own set
Of indelible
Lasting impressions.
Stringing these together

Creates a motion
As a nurturing breeze
Which nudges one along,
Towards a destiny
Why you have come here
To accept with dignity
An honourable designation.
As you breathe, so
Do you then absorb
By each inhalation
A caving, caring current.

Harmonic Hues

Your son can still hear you
As he still exists
If anything
His senses are heightened.
It seems to you
There is a barrier
Is all in your mind
As he visits you each day.
There in your presence
As you have let
This to be known;
As only in body.
Is he absent
He's near in spirit
This should bring peace
To a lonely heart.
Accidents happen
Have to live and let live
As he knows your pain,
Yet in the same breath.
He doesn't want you to lose
A single second
With those you can still touch
These are his thoughts,
Which he wants me to share
So ones still in your midst
Friends and family
Can bring each other comfort.
Can't be in misery

Happiness can be had
If you are open
To its embracing warmth.
A tenderness
Awaits your reply
There are degrees of closeness
Do not be missing out on,
What stares you in the face
Love has so many shades
Each has a different light
To endow you with harmonic hues.

Stay Within Reason

I am here forever
Not just two more years
Won't be all smooth sailing
Such is the nature of life.
What I do expect
Is to always be near
Not far out of earshot
What a father is,
This I intend to be
So when you need me
Have one to depend on
Who is only,
An arm's length away
So if you happen
To come upon
A bump in the road,
Which you can't handle
Then I can step in
To provide guidance
To help you navigate.
To give you an out
To grasp an angle
That was elusive
To become fluent.
To believe in yourself
To have a sense of calm
To stay within reason
On an even keel.
These are the attributes

Which come into shape
The more you experience
Personal challenges.
By telling the truth
You stay on the side
Where others have trust
In what you do and say.
People need to know
You have integrity
The root of all interactions
To move in a forward direction.

Humble Beginnings

Every time I went by
This one certain tree
I felt a pull
I was being drawn.
The first few times
I could have been mistaken
But not after that
As this intelligence,
Through a telepathy
So communicated
With my higher spirit
Who translated for me,
That I was to attend
At my earliest convenience
To touch the roots
Of my ancestors.
I had always sensed
A close connection
With a sentient earth
But this was beyond,
What I ever imagined
To think I was aligned
With the intricacy
On an interwoven thread,
I was not shocked
But I was intrigued
So I went as asked
Just followed my instincts.
I trusted the breeze

To let flow these notes
Upon my breath
To be immersed within,
As with any symmetry
There is a cycle
So what I sent out
Was then in time returned.
By this interaction
I became more lucid
As to the depths
Of my humble beginnings.

Second Atmosphere

A world within a world
An earth inside our earth
Beneath the layers
A second atmosphere.
Life as we know it
So far beyond
An expansive nature
Through the stratas.
Species long extinct
Alive and well
Crystals chiming
In homeostasis.
A rare orchid
A timeless beauty
An ancient wisdom
Shared among life forms.
A place devoid
Of lesser traits
Of anger, hatred or envy
Only higher aspirations.
To gain entrance
One needs to be
Of an order
An enlightened entity.
When in their midst
What avails itself
Is a serenity
Which silently surrounds.
A calming presence

Inundates softly
From shallows to depths
All points in between.
A synergy
Fills each living length
By its universal chi
Of dripping droplets.
A sustenance
All roots merge from one
Not entangled
In synchronistic symmetry.

Telling River

As smart as you get
You never stop learning
Each day is a lesson
If you are open to it.
Each drop of rain
Every ray of light
Has a sentient component
To be nurtured.
We are not here
For the sake of
Just existing
Our surface is,
As an iceberg
Far more below
But to fully access
We must embrace all sides.
In an equal manner
Truth and consequences
Are so embedded
Within our mosaic.
This web that we weave
Is an intricate design
Each thread has significance
Vital meaning,
To why and where
We are at each moment
Can't just go through the motions
Comprehension,
Is a necessity

In order to decipher
Which then enables
Us to evolve,
Hence the reason
Why we never cease
Not only breathing
But interpreting signs,
In the wonders of life
If we dangle our feet
In this telling river
So will the current reveal its secrets.

Ageless Exuberance

I've never forced anyone
To be with me
Or to do something
They did not wish.
If they were inspired
And we both agreed
Then a collaboration
Would have proceeded.
So taken place
Under mutual skies
For this coming together
Then was a dream come true.
If there was blue in both
Not a frigidness
Then a warmth enabled
Would have one flicker lit.
My heart has always
Been near to that
Of my dear departed mother
My soul as eternal,
As life itself
I have walked many paths
I have endured danger
As well have been in love.
The essence of my spirit
Is free of any reins
My voice unbridled
My reason, uncompromised.
People come from

Distant origins
We are all star forms
Although most fail,
To recognize
Themselves in their
True glowing light
I embrace myself,
What I represent
The little boy
Inside of the man
An ageless exuberance.

Step

A step down can
Be viewed as a step up
It's not contradictory
For when one's humble,
It's like you're walking
When always driving
See images you glanced
In finer detail.
As your tempo slows
Life is less of a blur
Begin to appreciate
What's in your midst.
Puts your head on straight
When it was contorted
Learn what's really important
Imagine that.
This prepares you for
What's coming next
Not getting ahead of yourself
Catching up to the times,
Find what you wouldn't have
Had you continued
Along the same path
But by shifting gears,
You're able to grasp
What previous to
Slipped between your fingers
Being always in,
An all fired rush

When you take a moment
To smell the roses
Their essence inundates.
Then on your next outing
By your last experience
You wish to be
Beside waters,
Which are serene
By this full exposure
You sense and feel
The beauty you were meant to attract.

One Latitude

I've been quiet long enough
In this day and age
Of emancipation
I will speak my peace,
That as a species
We are far behind
Other life forms we consider
To be below us,
First off this mis-conception
Is a deep error
As we all belong
On one latitude,
There is an equilibrium
Then actually
Our so called instincts
Due to their non-use,
Have so suffered
To our own detriment
When those having to survive
Are on the cutting edge.
Others know when
As their senses reveal
A true reality
To stay or vacate an area,
Before a threat
Presents itself
By being in touch
With an inner rhythm.

We are all born with
These inherent abilities
If such collect dust
Upon a shelf,
They will not respond
As are designed
For the simple reason
Of a lethargic pulse.
The will to exercise
To reach our potential
So a function
Can serve its purpose, is paramount.

Iron Resolve

The loss of a gentle soul
This visionary
A life stolen
Before his time.
He who was persecuted
Due to his ideals
One of a stature
Held in high regard.
Kept in seclusion
As his following
Encouraged expression
Which was forbidden.
As his last breath
Sets upon him
So does this passing
Make him a martyr.
More influential
In spirit than in body
Voices won't be silenced
They are awakened.
A wrong committed
Has only served
As a rallying point
To strengthen a sinew.
Threats and intimidation
Work on the weak minded
This has stiffened
An iron resolve.
Lives may be lost

More will come in their place
As a people are not
Meant to be put asunder.
War is not the answer
Vigilance to stand
To face a dictator
As each person is sovereign.
As they place their roses
In solemn memory
Of a courageous leader
His cause won't be forgotten.

To honour the memory of Alexei Navalny

Temples Of Your Soul

Have an ear to the ground
Are down to earth
A fluid motion
From an inner stream.
You who are of
Infinite ancient clans
As one so ends
Then another begins.
Each is an extension
In you is the constant
Never cease to exist
Are a collection,
Of indelible marks
Which you leave behind
Not to be remembered by
But heard in silence.
When pieced together
A string is made
Of a continuous echo
A bridge between,
An evolving frequency
Pushes forward
Segments to a foundation
Pillars in your own Stonehenge.
Each on its own
Is similar, yet unique
But when their vibrations
Are blended into one.
This causes cosmic shifts

For by these changing
Tectonic plates
Kingdoms rise and fall.
But what remains fluent
Is the light within
Each window pane
That shines upon,
Which is a source
Of everlasting chi
So dwells around
The temples of your soul.

Miracle Of Existence

This earth is alive
A giver of life
She does embody
The miracle of existence.
In perfect alignment
For exact proximity
In distance from the sun
For photosynthesis.
Not too hot or cold
As absolute extremes
Would simply negate
The possibility.
Here as it seems
Dreams are realized
From north to south
From east to west.
Along ley lines
Do spiritual sites
Such as Stonehenge
Come into being.
In streams of consciousness
A knowingness circulates
For those of a cognizance
Such raises their vibration.
As she breathes, we breathe
When she nurtures
We're the recipients
Of her kindness.
We need to reciprocate

Yet most do the opposite
So use and abuse
Unequal principles.
I listen to her thoughts
As there will come a day
When even her resilience
Will be pushed beyond the limits.
My hands are placed
To send through my channel
A sustaining sustenance
As she so loves so do I in return.

Silver Lining

Just give this a chance
Let the forces at work
Weave their magic
All is not lost.
You may just find
A silver lining
Inside a reflection
From your beautiful smile.
You wanted a change
This has been granted
With the condition
That you give an effort,
Which this deserves
So means to plant a seed
See this blossom
If nurtured by your light.
It is the big picture
As you turn this page
Which now requires
You to come of age.
There's no looking back
Only forward
With a courage
An indomitable spirit.
Just take the step
Without any fear
Don't forget the past
But remember,
What got you here

This is the attitude
That will not relinquish
Believes in a better tomorrow.
Have much more within
Than you have a clue about
Slow down and breathe
Think before you act,
It's amazing
What so happens
When you are calm
So begin to comprehend.

Horizon

Did what couldn't be done
According to whom
Those in the know
Then this was equal,
To a revelation
A pleasant reminder
When you defy the odds
This goes against the grain.
So you made your own
Why go with what's common ?
You in your wisdom
Found an alternate route.
Lending credence
That there's more than one way
To see this happen
It's one thing to believe,
Another totally
To manifest itself
In the real world
By your creativity.
You delved and found
The needle in the haystack
Twisted and turned
At every angle.
This flexibility
The ability
To adapt when
In tight corners,
Has seen you through

The eye of a storm
As you've come up with
Not only what's plausible,
But fits seamlessly
As although you changed tracks
You made this appear
As if this was normal,
When nothing is
Farther from the truth
As you went to such lengths
So expanded your horizons.

No Two

No two are the same
Be it an interest
Or a certain belief
Why each has their own drum.
No two sound exactly
There are slight differences
Be this in octave
Or its projection.
May speak the same language
But with variations
It's in the vibration
Unique to the self.
No two end up
At one certain place
As their starting points
May vary considerably.
The reason then for
Why we are at
This moment in time
Is our individuality.
Each has their wheel
No two like another
All have their destination
To fulfill their destiny.
Two may have a background
Which appears similar
But their experiences
Define the person.
On any given day

On a particular street
Two may cross paths
Each with their version.
As the flow of thoughts
Channel through their streams
No two depictions
Are on one frequency.
With our diversity
Try to share neutral ground
Where consensus
Is a forethought, not an after-thought.

Integrity

It's time for me
To look at my life
What do I dream of ?
Where do I want to be ?
I have to realize
The only route to get there
Is by my ambitions
Not on other's coat tails.
The fun and games
Must slowly be replaced
With a mature attitude
My future rests,
On my shoulders
I'd have this no other way
I have it within
To make this happen.
This means my priorities
Need to be shuffled
From top to bottom
As I wish success.
This comes at a price
I have been told
Now I'm reminding myself
To start looking,
At this world I'm in
With an evolved vision
To leave the shallows
To enter the depths.
Ready or not

I have to test the waters
To stay buoyant
But also to flourish.
To have an appreciation
For what lies ahead
I will myself immerse
In these currents,
For therein are
The challenges
Which I come face to face
That I'll meet with determined integrity.

Time

Time waits for nobody
Just be in line
If you procrastinate
So get left behind.
As the minutes tick by
You have yourself
To credit or blame
For your gain or loss.
Can't pass the buck
As seasons come and go
It's you and you only
Who can change the script.
It is humbling
To be at the mercy
Of the crystals
In an hour glass.
A dose of reality
Brings us back down to earth
If we thought for one second
Others were at,
Our beck and call
Well no one is
A rude awakening
As our past comes home to roost.
Begin to piece
The parts together
As the wind so sings
Whispers truth in our ears.
To get up in the morning

To have a good night's sleep
So that we're able
To have the will,
To shape our day
As to waste a moment
Is a chance you can never
Get to recoup from.
So going forward
If you wish no regrets
Take the bull by the horns
Create what you envision.

First Place

Don't like to make waves
I do when I have to
When it's a last resort
If I've exhausted,
All avenues
Then and only then
Do I put my foot down
To cease and desist.
I won't let this fester
To become more than
It already is
So nip this in the bud.
I go with the flow
Until I am forced
To do otherwise
When I have no choice,
But to respond
In a manner
Meets fire with fire
To douse the flames.
Not to enhance
So minimize
What caused this in the first place
To not have a repeat.
Can tolerate
To a certain point
When this is reached
Just have to intervene.

Do the unpopular thing
At times in life
We find ourselves
Between a rock,
And a hard place
In such a bind
That in order to loosen
We go against our grain.
Just to remove a slide
That makes a better door
Than a window
To once again traverse freely.

Songbird

To be free at last
It is a blessing
To be without pain
As her quality of life,
Made this existence
Especially near the end
Difficult to bear
With the constant aches.
How she is endeared
How she will be missed
The voice of a songbird
The love of a dear sister.
Yes you will be missed
But in the same breath
We are forever grateful
Your suffering is over.
You whose sparkle
Is an inspiration
To each of us
We will carry,
This light within
With pride and honour
As knowing you
Was like being acquainted,
With an angel
As you ascend
Those stairs to the beyond
Your wings begin to glisten.
Can hear you laughing

As you once did
To us this brings comfort
Sharing such a vision.
You will be remembered
From all the times
In so many moments
We were in your presence.
Each is cherished
There is no distance
As a closeness remains
The lines between stay open.

In loving memory of Sharon

Inner Temple

Let your breath expand
Slowly seep in
To the farthest reaches
Of your entire being.
Through these channels
A rushing river
Replenishes
A nutrient wave.
By each inhalation
So cleanse and remove
That which would block
The smallest airway.
This ounce of prevention
Is worth more than
A pound of cure
Such extends your lifespan.
For what you see
Transcends this realm
As that which touches
Your inner temple,
Is of a purity
So only lengthens
By a natural rhythm
Whose cycle renews,
This regeneration
As in you is no friction
Just a placid
Continuation.
This which you practice

Is more, not less
Endows your system
With a fluidness.
Each revolution
Enhances this flow
As more is learned
Then is applied,
To the following turn
By such absorption
An ever present aura
Evolves in a circular pattern.

Tickety-Boo

I am transported
When I listen
To vibrational music
As this crosses,
The membranes between
Alternate dimensions
By being this placid
Such enables,
One to focus
On a single thought
Blocking out the
Superfluous.
All in one motion
As the wheels move
I'm in transition
From here to there.
When I get where I'm going
I'm tickety-boo
All warm inside
From a pleasant journey.
This re-programs
My entire pattern
As with calmness in hand
All is possible.
The creativity
Goes off the charts
Being an open channel
The stars are infinite.
Their sparkles shimmer

Along the pathway
Inside of a tunnel
To the outer cosmos.
This connects the dots
In a constellation
Whose auspicious image
Manifests radiance.
I am transformed
From my chrysalis
I emerge as
A golden dragonfly.

23 Legacy

When we come into this world
It's not with what
Are empty chambers
Far from this in fact.
As we are an
Accumulation
Of all of our past lives
With the most recent,
Still bubbling on our surface
As we aren't one and done
We have a legacy
With multiple extensions.
Most we can remember
As if they were yesterday
Some we'd wish to forget
Each has its own niche.
A reason to be
Which then translates
Sewn into the mosaic
As this is our story,
With complementing themes
A continuation
As when recognition
Puts the pieces together,
Then we have moments
Of clairvoyance
As insight elucidates
To bind the pages,
Then a light that was flickering

Becomes more constant
To illuminate
A steady stream.
As visions engage
With our memories
They become so vivid
As to place us back,
To when they first occurred
But the only difference
By this blending
We comprehend the shades in between.

Those Of The Time

The more evidence
Which filters through
Greater is the consensus
Some civilizations,
On our sacred earth
Were far advanced
Thousands of years ago
Which now lie beneath the waves.
A form of levitation
That lifted heavy stones
As if they were a feather
Such knowledge of the ancients,
Was common among
Those of the time
Quite readily shared
To erect esoteric structures.
Who were looked upon
By native clans
As some kind of deities
Who flew chariots in the sky.
Accorded high esteem
As some out of fear
Others just believing
These were their saviours.
Each had their own belief
As to where they were from
Or their reason
For being there at that time.
If they'd known the truth

It may have been a comfort
Seeing a peaceful integration
If this was their experience.
These distant cultures
As primitive as they were
Had signs of spirituality
Which was faithfully practised.
Why the cloud people
Came here in the first place
This planet holds such promise
With a horizon full of wisdom.

Cosmic Coronation

To be in the presence of
This dawning spectacle
Was a magical moment
As this solar eclipse,
So unfolded
Before my very eyes
In a sacred place
On the shores of Superior.
As the moon moved in front
Inching as a sea shell
Shadows emerged
So did a gravitational pull,
See the tide recede
Waters exposed stones
At the wrong time of day
This was all nature,
Showing in subtle gestures
Even affecting sleeping patterns
For those who work with
Constant flows of light.
I could feel myself
In this effervescence
Slowly augmenting
Through its rotation.
For as I am part of her
She is that in me
A reciprocal
Enduring bond.
As the sun's surface

Was nearly covered
My temples bubbled
By this cosmic coronation.
I was mesmerized
By the magnificence
Of what transpired
Closer than I actually was.
Such is the power
Of the magnification
Of two cerebral orbs
Coming into a brief alignment.

Revealing Dawn

This is a new beginning
As the sun rises
In the early morning
A warmth exudes,
Which has replaced
A faded image
As a crisp night air
Acquiesces to,
This promising orb
Ascending in the east
Whose rays transcend
Towards the metaphysical.
I stand in its path
With open arms
Embracing a destiny
I have awaited.
That had been foretold
To my spirit
Before my entry
Into this current stream.
I take my first steps
Into the light
Here is serenity
In its purest form.
It's like I'm being pulled
A little at a time
In a direction
With a resonance.
I have an inclination

As to what I will find
When I get to where I'm going
Why this beacon,
Only becomes stronger
The closer I near
This destination
Which I'm soon upon.
I approach a clearing
With a revealing dawn
Through cosmic emanations
I reach my metamorphosis.

Expand Your Wings

There will come a day
Some point down the road
When you'll feel different
Than as you do now.
For the better, not worse
As your priorities
Will naturally evolve
As you begin,
The initial ascent
Upon your mountain
As the innocence fades
Is replaced by,
This set of core values
Which will stay attached
For the duration
Of this precious life.
As you are at present
May not this person
Either recognize
Or identify with,
When you're older
As you grow by stages
So become more complex
Less thinking about the one,
More concerned with the whole
A change in perspective
Sees the heart and mind
Merge in a synthesis.
Your personal views

Are in for a shift
From the singular
To a plurality.
An enhanced vision
Will broaden your horizons
To comprehend
What's currently,
Beyond your grasp
But not in the future
As this vocabulary
Will expand your wings.

Edge Of Tomorrow

It is not the physical
But the spiritual side
Which becomes more vibrant
Once this shell is gone.
As this life represents
One revolution
A single full circle
A page in your book.
These inhalations
See us be like a sponge
As we merge with
The parts that we touch.
As the breeze extends
Its influence
So do we expand
Our own horizons,
Within our reach
Is the recognition
That we are beyond
Being mere mortals.
In our thought patterns
Are higher ideals
These we channel
Like streams of water.
As they funnel through
There is constant
Current revisions
Which enhance our cosmology.
These evolving strands

Change our outlook
From being in the moment
To living on,
The edge of tomorrow
This is where we
Can bring to the field
A fertile plane.
In which to flourish
As it's only by
Such replenishing
That our stems rejuvenate.

Signs And Symbols

A world is out there
That is far more
Than most would believe
Could ever be true.
But the evidence
Is all around us
If we only
Take our heads out of the sand.
As ignorance can be
A safety blanket
But in this day and age
Of transparency,
The signs and symbols
Are hard to eschew
Like defying gravity
Truth is ever present.
Some would attempt
To this conceal
As knowledge is power
And the stones tell a story.
As do the trees
For those who care to listen
Such an abundance
Of non-coincidental facts.
Literally
The writings are on the walls
Of ancient structures
Which were left behind,
For interpretation

Etchings and language
Of eras gone by
That instilled a brilliance.
As the stars can speak
A sparkle diminished
By ones not wanting to share
A sentience meant,
To be ubiquitous
Secrets preserved
In broad daylight
To enlighten the less privileged.

Perfect Resonance

Can I be open with you ?
There will be days
Along the way
When you won't know,
Which direction to turn
When you're at a crossroads
As doubt intervenes
As to where you should be,
On such occasions
You don't want to be active
But rather quiet
For haste makes waste.
A decision then
Will cause future regret
As you want a clear mind
When you make a choice.
To be on sturdy ground
Not a shaky surface
Sure of yourself
Not flipping a coin.
In between a rock
And a hard place
When you feel pinched
It's not the right time,
To dowse for answers
A little patience shown
Will prove the wisest
For when you're at peace,
Intuitions are revealed

Not in a heightened state
But in serene moments
When your temples aren't tight.
As you want to be loose
Calm and collected
Then you can receive
Messages from within.
As you delve deeper
The reasons reflect
A perfect resonance
Of elucidation.

Mother

For all the mothers
Present and departed
For Pachamama
For dear grandmothers,
This is a tribute
To recognize
A life well lived
To a commitment,
To your children
Who have grown up
Instilled with values
Who know words are not meaningless.
That when you say something
This has substance
Not for a day
But for eternity.
As love transcends
All lives and dimensions
It does not cease to exist
In the hearts of those,
Who know the depths
Of compassion
To be there in times
Of happiness and sadness.
Who never let go
Of a caring hand
Or let slip through their fingers
The enduring one.
Here is gratitude

For having given
Freely of yourselves
Without receiving expectations.
As a child born unto you
Will always be yours
If loved and nurtured
With unending patience.
As the bonds between
Last further and beyond
A single walk tenure
Why we remember and smile.

Messengers

Messengers from beyond
Have in the past
Made their presence felt
Such was true for yesterday.
I've been thinking about
A journey to Greece
Here's where the synchronicity
So began in earnest,
On the afternoon of the same day
I received my
Baseball playing jersey
Whose number seventy-seven,
I chose myself
While walking the dog
At the park by the river
I saw silhouettes,
In white wispy clouds
One of the ways
Spirits communicate with me
The first two shapes,
Were the numerals
I had specified
So their telepathy
Reached my receptors.
The last symbol
Was a smiling dolphin
Saying the time is now
The door is open.
While driving home

Once more there was a formation
Which appeared as
A check mark no less,
With a face at the small point
Strongly resembling
That of the Greek God Zeus
I was told in,
No uncertain terms
That a sphere of light
Would be waiting at Delphi
To raise my ascension.

Language From The Stars

As you begin to drift off
What first comes to mind
Is a pleasing tunnel
Filled with emerald shades.
This means of course
You are in for
A period of
Surging enhancement.
An oasis appears
You try to interpret
But as you're immersed
Your vibration shifts,
To a higher octave
Where the once invisible
Suddenly becomes
Quite conspicuous.
As you have given
Freely of yourself
So do you now receive
A just return,
As you go deeper
More than ever before
What comes into sight
Is miraculous,
A flow of ideas
Which were once foreign
Are now second-hand
Due to being endowed.
By an encounter

With an intelligence
That is far above
Our own species.
As this filters
Through your sentient dream
You converse in a language
Of numbers and symbols.
A new part of you
Is slowly awakened
Once seen, twice as fluent
In a knowledge from the stars.

Face To Face

I told two a story
About what transpired
A week ago
A magical experience,
Little did I know
The sparkle in the moment
Was a dream that I
Wished to share with one of them.
For when I relayed
Seeing myself
Going to a pyramid
In mystical Egypt,
Having a door open
Then re-acquainting
My current being
With a previous life,
The catch of this all
Was the name Akhenaten
For then both caught on
As to the importance.
This is when she
Came out with it
That my former life entity
Was no other,
Than one of her
Protective spirit guides
This revelation
On both of our parts,
Made for an instant

Bonding connection
Both being cognizant
Of the rarity,
Of this occurrence
As it formed a halo
Inside of which
Both could be found.
This meeting was scripted
No chance in this
As fate intervened
To bring us face to face.

Tantalizing Cusp

What stands in front of you
Is inspiration
Every reason
To make the most of,
What lies beneath your waves
For in this current
Is the passion and means
To propel you to become,
Go to your highest height
To realize that inside
Is where you will find
That push to touch your dreams.
As there in the midst
Is a burning flame
The light that you are
Which needs to breathe.
This air in your sails
Will only be sustained
If you draw upon
A recurring cycle.
It's all in place
Just by instinct
Will you know how and when
To usher in the wind.
As the trickles begin
The first inhalation
Creates a brisk breeze
That fills a void.
This empty space

Now takes on the shape
Of a vibrant
Life pursuing ambition.
On the coming horizon
You are on the verge
Of a tantalizing cusp
That illuminates,
A pristine path
For yours is outside
But fully within
The scope of one's cosmology.

As Far – As High

I long for those days
Of youthful innocence
Not a worry
In a wonderful world.
A time when not knowing
The weight of life
Let me float as a feather
In a serene meadow.
Not as a busy bee
But as a child upon
An untouched beauty
When everything glittered.
When I believed
There was good in all
At least for a while
Until my orbs evolved.
Which would happen soon enough
Like living a dream
My own reality
Without the darkness.
When my eyes danced
In anticipation
Of what tomorrow
Would bring with its sunrise.
Most often being outside
In touch with nature
Running and jumping
As far, as high,
As could possibly be

Smiling and laughing
To be where and as you were
To feel lucky,
To know how fortunate
To be growing up
Devoid of fear
Not going hungry.
Fast forward to now
Want to re-live those moments
To cherish in memory
To spread its magical dust upon today.

Spheres Of Influence

Our beautiful earth
She who absorbs
Our toxicity
An empath of our thoughts.
She who is cognizant
Of all that transpires
Within and around
The realms of these corners.
As we are living
And conscious beings
Our benefactor's depths
Are beyond our comprehension.
Few have realized
Her complexity
As these spheres of influence
Are infinite,
In their resolve
These plants and trees
Are of a sentience
Is higher than our own.
As we see life
One creates the means
To so enable
Our existence.
To put this in terms
We are here at the
Generosity
Of an altruistic entity.
We use her land, air and waters

Are her inhabitants
Not in reverse
So deserves our respect.
When I say namaste
It is with a gratitude
To be permitted
For we are as her children.
This is the relationship
Which stands between
As I look up and outward
I embrace her warmth and kindness.

Resuscitate

Resuscitate
Replenish the soul
Rejuvenate
Re-light the lamp.
Empower boldly
Enlighten the spirit
Evolve in a hue
Enhances intuition.
Think before you speak
Treat others as if
They are your inner-self
Trust your instincts.
Be confident
Believe in your path
Brighten the stones
Beneath your waters.
Let the wind in your sails
Levitate you beyond
Lifting you higher
Leading to a summit,
Where you observe
White cylindricals
Wispy, wiry clouds
Wanting to reveal,
Impressions of nature
Inspiring portals
Involving like spheres'
Illuminations.
Opening their doors

On mystical moments
Observing shared visions
One spectacle at a time.
As you stand atop
Another silver strand
Attaches itself
After a face to face,
Crystals encircling
Coming together
Complementing striations
Colourful constellations.

Branch Out

This circling pattern
Is in for a change
As you are on the verge
Of an about face,
As the center you
Will begin to branch out
To think beyond
The confines of,
Your limiting sand box
On the day when this happens
It will be like
You are struck by lightning.
What comes over
Will be second nature
Which before was
Unattainable,
All in a matter
Of removing the walls
Had prevented you from
Seeing the light of day.
As the streams reach your eyes
These liberating rays
Are the key which
Unlocks the door,
As a dam is burst
A sudden rush
May at first overwhelm
But you will adapt.
In short order

As this ability
Lies deep within
Each one of us.
You are no different
An inward spiral
Has a hold until we
Are touched by an influence,
This being an illumination
So becomes visible
When we are close to enter
The intuitive stage of our life.

One Fell Swoop

I invited a robin
To nest in a tree
Then it did just that
Will take this as an omen.
First off I was heard
Second that my words
Were acted upon
In one fell swoop.
A close affinity
Brought us together
From the earth beneath
To the sky above.
Then all in between
Her eyes are upon me
I'm never alone
As this love is eternal.
To be side by side
Still free, yet near at hand
As the story continues
So too does the bond.
This only affirms
What I've always believed
More does exist
Outside of this realm.
Not independent of
But in proximity
Sees us almost share
The exact same space,
Breathing a common air

So as the bird flies
So do I journey
Along an aligned path.
In synchronicity
By the moment
Is this then enhanced
By an inner beacon.
Which evolves as do we
Without any thought
Purely by instinct
In an accorded rhythm.

Origin Of Our Dreams

Each day has a lesson
If we are open to it
If we let go of the past
That weighs us down.
To keep chips on your shoulder
Puts up a barrier
That will always exist
Until you move beyond,
This in itself
Is a turning point
One, not all reach
For some reason,
Or another
These teachings are
There to be had
To bring us forward.
We often stand in the way
Of our own progression
As the truth can be
At times the last,
That we want to hear
But the very words
Which can motivate
Us out of our dormancy.
The purpose of this
Is to touch the dawn
Whose trickle effect
Sees a change occur.
This is deeply rooted

Those with the ability
To adapt will survive
Plain and simple.
To absorb is to flourish
To listen, to integrate
With our own morals
Creates a life journey.
This road is what
We make it to be
No more, no less
From within is derived the origin of our dreams.

Wavelength

I am the way I am
For who loved me
When I was a child
Whose heart shines on mine.
My tiny sparkle
Had its beginnings
In her tender arms
Flowing from a humble chamber.
I was enchanted
As she showered me with
A ring of shooting stars
Which remain to this day.
A lasting effect
A warmth that perseveres
Throughout all seasons
And all the years.
I'm forever grateful
For the times we share
As even in spirit
I feel her presence.
So there is no end
Just continuity
A smile this brings
Still feeling her near.
Knowing inside
That no matter what
I can myself transcend
As her halo appears.
A comfort from beyond

No fences or doors
Just an open plane
To share a closeness once more.
As I'm right here
She is over there
We bridge the distance
By strengthening a wavelength.
As long as I remember
The light in the lamp
Will keep its flicker
As bright as can be.

Depths To Which You've Been

Please walk among them
Although they're invisible
To the naked eye
These spirits still persist.
You were and still are
Of a select clan
Which practised channeling
At such you were adept.
You each come back
On your own time lines
To live this karmic path
That is your chosen field.
You hear this calling
Like an echo
Across a valley
Inside this evokes,
A destiny
In incremental steps
One foot, then the next
This follows from,
Your flowing instincts
Can even close your eyes
Will yet end up where
You are meant to be.
You're part of the visionaries
Who long ago
Were so endowed
With senses beyond.
Still putting this together

But the further you go
Becomes more evident
The depths to which you've been.
You have come around
On different worlds
In various life forms
To fulfill your purpose.
Your current stream
Has you returning
To familiar grounds
To re-acquaint yourself with a former existence.

One Constellation

Now that I'm going to Greece
See what transpires
As the coming
Interactions,
Will help me find
A sky without a ceiling
I have to go
The pull is that strong.
I have no expectations
Neither do I think
This happens on its own
Is manifested,
By the spirit
Inside of the person
If there is passion
Then this culminates,
In the realization
Of a nearing dream
As the thoughts begin
Its implementation,
Only comes about
With a commitment
To a process
Which sends this forward.
I have an idea
But this is so below
The actual potential
Yet one must start somewhere.
No better place or time

Than the here and now
The current in the present
Is an active beacon.
I embrace change
In this evolution
Will I grow in mind and soul
To merge with the ancients.
Of whom I am one
Although being young in heart
I too have lived other lives
The threads from which now create one constellation.

Ways Of Our Waves

You never cease to exist
A body is a shell
Short term rental
One's spirit is eternal.
Each life is poignant
In a line of succession
We are the totality
Of our passages.
No two are the same
Each has its reason
At a specific time
For coming into being.
Nothing is by accident
We are a living script
From which we document
The ways of our waves.
We follow along
Our input is vital
As we're at the helm
Whose current depends,
On our inner will
If we have it within
For self-determination
To plant the seed,
Then see it grow
From the beginning
Through to its destination
With love and light.
There is no ending

We don't go super nova
This is a journey
Which has segments,
Each is independent
But yet in the same breath
These eyes are perpetual
Yet know many shades.
The colours of which
Match those in our skies
So change as we evolve
From one life to the next one above.

Paths To My Lineage

When I return
A story will be told
One for the ages
About a prophecy.
As I do not forget
That who I am
Try to live up to
Paths to my lineage.
Numerous reflections
Shimmer upon these waters
Images of recollection
Pool inwards toward,
A lucid cognition
As a root extends
Like chapters in a book
Or links in a chain.
I go to the edge
Peer into the river
From faces in a capsule
Hear a unifying voice.
Which the ripples amplify
As it is time
To take the plunge
To find the access,
Beneath the surface
An intuition
Pulls me under
Near to an opening.
I knew this somehow

Like the back of my hand
As I enter
So am I welcomed.
This only intensifies
My past is explained
In its entirety
I am bound by these pages.
Although not the same person
Are one continuous
Vibrant entity
Closing in on my purpose.

Reach Within

To know yourself
To live life in moderation
Precepts of Apollo
To be enduring.
Hear what's being said
Inside the message
To be interpreted
With specific intent.
To comprehend
By your time present
To lead by example
In every facet.
The path behind
The tunnel ahead
Each in relation
An extension of the other.
To enter within
A clear, conscious mind
To focus upon
The task at hand.
That here in front of you
Is a moment
Worth remembering
For its salience.
The steps today
Will create tomorrow
As this wisdom
You begin to integrate.
So start to climb

Ever so slowly
An inch at a time
Towards a light,
That on this morning
Shines down brilliantly
Through its revealing rays
As a promise is fulfilled.
So have you the means
By a shared insight
To rise above
So reach and touch the moon.

A Love Of Song

The faces of a people
Connected by
A love of song
Beaming from a park at night.
A sky becomes alive
Pushing out through the universe
With a resounding
Dance of the mystics.
A land of mythology
Enhanced by storytellers
Who keep the embers burning
Of a romantic history.
Of battles won and lost
Of names remembered
Whose descriptions
Are etched in sweet memory.
So sing with every breath
Let the words rejoice
Reminding you of a time
So long ago,
As if it was yesterday
Fresh in your minds
Yet to an outsider
I feel the warmth,
The beauty of a culture
Sparkling in your eyes
When shared together
So flows in a circle.
What was, what still is

This dwells in your hearts
Put my hand up to the breeze
Surrounds me with,
A melody
A signature
A reason to behold
A trust to believe,
That in this country of Greece
Is a mark of old
A moral fibre
A sinew that binds us all.

Blessed

On the return ferry
From the island of Delos
I stood by the railing
On the lower deck,
To get more fresh air
From the Mediterranean Sea
Whose shades of blue
Inspire one's imagination.
The deep hues to turquoise
Blending together
In seamless striations
By this was I mesmerized.
I thought there and then
In days of old
On ancient wooden ships
How they traversed,
These same waters
How almost time stands still
Throughout history
Shaped by humans and nature.
I was nearly dreaming
When a splashing spray
Caught me by surprise
I knew I was endowed,
A woman saw me drenched
Said, " you have been blessed "
At that very moment
I shared her sentiments.
It was magical

An extension of
The experience I had
While walking upon,
The spiritual spaces
Of Gaia and Apollo
As if I was
Sent a message,
That coupled with The Oracle Of Delphi
I was now activated
Memories from my past
Now in harmony with my present.

Antiparos Cave

To go into the earth
Down her staircase
This winding path
Of a colourful past.
These stalactites
Suspended from the top
Of this ornate cavern
Of natural history.
The stories she can tell
Of terrafirma creation
By placing one's fingers
Upon these minerals.
There is a reaction
As you feel the vibe
Of millions, if not billions
Of years in transition.
You get a sense
By becoming
Intertwined with
This personification.
As she is alive
This is her footprint
As you step into
These ancient fissures.
Can feel as she does
Knows through experience
When will be the next tremor
As she lives and breathes,
With her roots embedded

To the very core
The inner rim
Of a constant heart beat.
These vibrant tentacles
Are in touch, are in reach
Of an emitting pulse
To which you've an affinity.
As you begin to ascend
In the early stage
So start to comprehend
Yourself within the walls of these crystals.

Sunrise

You are more serene
Your spirit has strengthened
Had the time of your life
Need to assimilate,
This higher vibration
As you're bubbling
Like a geyser
Can grasp intuition.
Was once above you
Now is right beside
As you humbly received
With gratitude,
What was waiting in place
As in your presence
Numbers were aligned
Are where you're meant to be.
These wings have rightly
Truly opened
Upon a plane
Is yours to be had.
With this ascension
Comes responsibility
A morality
Which all light workers governs.
Such you assume
With a dignity
You are known for
Why you were called.
This was the moment

Your sevens were up
The next part of your purpose
Begins to manifest itself.
You came to this point
Due to an earned distinction
Being recognized
For this determination,
A perseverance
Through dogged adversity
Kept raising the bar
Until you reached this sunrise.

Two Steps At Once

Try to remember my dreams
As messages now follow
After these frequencies
Which I absorbed,
Takes time to adapt
Like levitating
Walking on water
Similar to both.
I am adjusting
To my augmentation
Took two steps at once
As three winds intertwine.
This gentle swirling
So lends itself
To a wider expanse
To a greater knowledge.
Are sweeping changes
Literally in my midst
Almost being uprooted
As these surroundings,
Are so above
From where I was
An ascended dimension
Is this plane of existence.
Senses are heightened
Instincts are sharpened
Enhanced capabilities
Let me pass through a gate.
Till now was off limits

With this endowment
I am well inside
These sights and sounds,
This stirring in my hands
I'm not overwhelmed
Just need to go slow
Let the process take effect.
This mountain range
Its valleys and streams
Are at a vibration
Now acclimatize myself to.

The Unknown

It's never over
As one breath ends
Just as soon the next begins
Not always a smooth transition,
But there is no fear
Of what some call the unknown
The genius of life
Is facing each day,
With a courage
That's indomitable
Just take what is given
Make the most of it.
By being flexible
Saves one a lot of grief
If too rigid
Can fall apart.
Like circles on a tree
One ring follows
The preceding
Until we become,
Part of the earth again
But our entity
Our energy imprint
This is eternal.
The knowledge we
So accumulate
This is passed on
In cerebral memory.
Why all is not lost

As long as we remember
The tools to retrieve
From our recent past,
Are left in place
This flicker burns
Incessantly
As one stage reflects,
Upon its closest in time
Looking for a reason
Why here at this moment ?
Then a dawn shines with sentience.

Spirit Within

Each day I find reason
To rise with the sun
In life is such beauty
Every way that I turn.
On the wing of a thought
The air beneath
Pushes from below
To elevate a hope.
One that each morning
On a single breath
Has the very means
To ascend its mountains,
Whose peaks are nearing
Ever closer
To a summit of dreams
Which dawns upon,
In a shining spectacle
So reflects a stream
Of radiance
Uncovers what was hidden.
As moments of realization
String together
A cognizance
Whose pieces form,
At first an outline
Then an image
Which signifies
An emergence.
A re-birth if you will

To integrate
Past with present
As an inhalation,
Coming from before
Transcends to the current
A merging of two seas
Becomes a single wave.
I remember
Who I was, who I am
I know who I will be
Spirit within is part of each horizon.

Enduring Fondness

Are more well rounded
From my time in Greece
As a confidence
Now belies my,
Every step
With an eye on
Taking this evolution
To the next dimension.
In a short time
Wonders were seen and had
A music resonates
As does a warmth,
From a kind shopkeeper
As I was keen
To reciprocate
Even initiate,
Contact with its people
Who made their mark
Upon a tender heart
Bringing me into their circle.
I too in turn
Was touched by a
Sparkling ambiance
Which enveloped my aura.
I look at life
Differently
With a calmer
More demure impression.
I came without

Expectations
I left having experienced
An altered metamorphosis.
I can honestly say
This was a paradise
Part of me stayed behind
As part of then came with myself.
An equal sharing
A tranquil circumstance
To keep in my soul
Memories of an enduring fondness.

Unseen

It is the unseen
Which you has evolved
Yes, you sensed a presence
The one and the same,
Is the reason why
You have gone from
Just intending
This to happen,
To being able
To make it so
Not only immersed
But realizing,
The fruits of your labours
This may not seem like much
But such a subtle change
Is a world of difference.
As you start to adapt
Like you have come upon
A realm of your own
That was waiting,
For you to answer
Well you have arrived
Not with pomp and circumstance
But with a noble soul.
Are on your way
As you begin to respond
To this stimuli
You are in a good place.
This vantage point

Pushes your potential
To be infinite
In its scope and purpose.
You're entering
A time of promise
After all you've endured
Have stayed the course.
Never lost faith
Always believed
By sticking to your principles
The path ahead would reveal itself as it has.

Enlightened Being

In a vision
I was high atop a hill
Overlooking the ocean
Still, serene waters,
Under a canopy
With eight round stones
With symbols on each one
To make a circle.
There would I spend
A length of time
Absorbing the ambiance
By each inhalation.
After what seemed
Like a short duration
I opened my eyes
To a revised reality.
Steps were to be taken
To affect this change
To an altered perspective
Along a poignant path.
I came upon
A door which was
Like a transcending portal
Filled with hues from,
An inspiring rainbow
In a rhythmic flow
I was encircled
Then each was embedded,
In an ascending line

Through my chakras
Once departing
I stood beneath,
This radiating orb
Through levitation
This raised my entity up
Into the midst,
Of a floating field
Where I was
Further transformed
Into an enlightened being.

One And The Same

I don't go in circles
I listen to the breeze
I trust my instincts
To guide my path.
I look before I step
I think about
Effects and consequences
Of my actions.
I have a conscience
As well as a heart
The two are one and the same
Two peas in a pod.
They go hand in hand
Not through the motions
In a deliberate manner
To seed the universe,
With what matters
So becoming
Now a lost art
But this can be revived.
In those who still believe
Who have the strength
As well as the vision
Not to be blinded,
By a world veiled
From its true identity
I stay as I was
In my previous lives,
Undaunted by coercion

Being resilient
Not tempted by avarice
Enamoured with the light.
Why I go forward
With reason and purpose
Keeping to my beliefs
In the sanctity of life.
Will never cast aside
Who I am or
What I represent
A renewed hope with the coming dawn.

Square In The Path

We don't just come around once
Do trees have one circle?
No, they have one for
Each year in this revolution.
We aren't any different
There is no stop sign
A pause for the cause
To respect your sights.
Then off you go
To your next adventure
One after the other
To an altered destination.
Due to the fact
We are all here to learn
If we do from our last lesson
Then up and outward,
Do we so evolve
To place this life
In its proper context
Following along,
A line of succession
Puts us square in the path
For an experience
To absorb sage from.
I like to think
There's more to this
Than what's on such a plane
A profound meaning.
Which is in front of my eyes

For when them I close
I truly start to see
To comprehend.
First I observe
These moving shadows
Then how dimensions
So interact.
When I piece this together
The universe becomes smaller
As I find my place within
This sentience calms my soul.

Fitting Embrace

My father has not been well
His time will soon be up
If I have , but one wish
I want to come true,
Is that dad lasts long enough
To see my son's first child
This would bring a joy
A sparkle to our eyes.
As sad as I am
That one life is almost over
A baby held in his arms
Will make his transition peaceful.
Miracles can happen
This would rank right up there
A fitting embrace
To tie opposite ends.
Will do what I can
So this can transpire
A touch from a hand
To span across.
To reach tiny fingers
With breaths remaining
So to peer into
These orbs of tomorrow.
Saying hello, not goodbye
As a memory
So created
Will endure for eternity.
An impression left

Will have an indelible mark
From which to remember
An early acquaintance.
Two from the same family
The elder and the newborn
A cause for reflection
From a shared ember.
One that will burn
Its pure essence
In the hearts and souls
Of the departed and those who stay on this plane.

Hope And Promise

Communication from beyond
Can happen when
You least expect it to
In the rarity,
Of an occurrence
Through symbolism
A nearing approach
Elicits a message.
That wisdom granted
Will soon have its dawn
To shine down upon you
In all of its brilliance.
In the form of a card
That seeks to divulge
To which few have access
As you have earned a trust.
Now going forward
You do so with
An unbridled courage
To grasp the unknown.
To not keep this to yourself
But to disseminate
To those less privileged
To help in any way possible.
The second part
Of this twin flame
Is that you'll receive
An ember of passion.
This could be in the shape of

An interest or woman
Only time will tell
Which comes to pass.
That missing link
Will find its chain
Be complete and fulfilled
In its totality.
The blank spaces
Will be a distant memory
As each day you rise
With hope and promise.

The Stars Above

The secret is out
What you're about
Too long kept silent
Just let it be known.
That you are one
From a rare breed
A heart with a soul
That shines constantly.
The rays from which
You direct to others
Without any
Thought of yourself.
This is you though
In a nut shell
Unselfish in your ways
As kind as kind can be.
What you think is nothing
Means everything
Out of the ordinary
A beacon of light.
Few and far between
Are those like yourself
Give without expecting
Anything in return.
You deserve so much
Don't like a fuss
If it's for you
Symmetry comes back.
You're dearly loved

Now and forever
This will only change
In its brilliance.
You are cherished
Every single day
Not just once a year
But each one throughout.
You make an impression
Upon those you touch
A lasting reflection
As you're from the stars above.

Second Vision

Just let yourself go
Be free of all constraints
Loosen the strings
Walk barefoot around.
Once you get your feet wet
Start to see life
With a different angle
As you catch on,
So comes a second vision
One with more depth
One whose liberation
Gives you access,
To higher knowledge
As your soles aren't toughened
But become attuned
To a sensitized pulse.
Now you are able
To put the pages
In their proper order
Like you were blind before.
As you proceed
You flawlessly pass through
One after the other
These stages of cognition.
Each with its own
Plane of poignance
Where are revealed
Symbolic vicissitudes.
As you interpret

As you adapt
Your rainbow's abundance
Expands its aura.
You wonder why
That at this time
Then you answer
Your own question.
Now at this juncture
You are ready to cross
To be immersed
Within a stream of akashic intuitions.

Higher Purpose

Since very young
I knew I was different
For I was kept here
Through spiritual intervention.
After two accidents
That were non-coincidental
So was I guided
To a higher purpose.
My path was chosen
In direct line
From my past life
To be an extension.
As a means to an end
Have been hills and valleys
Not a smooth transition
But then again,
This was part of the plan
That I stumble and fall
When I got back up
So would wisdom flow.
I've had my moments
I take full responsibility
For the one I've become
As a person.
I admit my faults
As well as my strengths
A little of both
Creates this symmetry.
The fact I continue

Is testimony
To the road laid out for me
Like an obstacle course.
So that later in life
Or early in the next
I will come face to face
With this destiny.
A combination
Of a hand from above
And a touch of free will
The two together is who I am.

Cycling Current

This present destination
Has come around slowly
To reveal by moonlight
A growing synthesis.
The early years
Were quite tight lipped
Just having to endure
Almost total silence.
As I got older
A few words were released
Enough to keep me going
On a few bread crumbs.
What I did receive
I made good use of
To so decipher
What was being said.
Encrypted messages
To nudge me along
At times gently
In others harshly.
Would all depend
If I was listening
Could not just be absorbed
But properly perceived.
So I meandered
As would a snail
Meaningful steps
Left their indentation.
Which I would not forget

They would jostle my memory
Leaving an asterisk beside
These dawning moments.
When pieced together
So would a reason
Find its inspiration
To come into being.
As I look back
As I peer forward
A ray shines on my temples
Illuminating a cycling current.

Ascendance

Came as you were asked
Exceeded in your steps
Careful not to disturb
Still left an imprint.
A delicate
Balancing act
Two seas merged as one
As two currents intertwined.
You found yourself
In familiar surroundings
Not from this life
But in that previous.
A re-acquaintance
As you heard the knock
Followed up by
Enticing sounds,
From a frequency
Whose emanations
Remained intact
From centuries before.
So like an old friend
Or even a past lover
A presence welcomed
Under every,
Type of circumstance
Like going back home
This place you knew
With a keen eye.
The day came and went

But it's what stayed
Within as a reminder
That sees you gravitate,
Toward a center
Hidden until now
In you was activated
The next stage of,
Your ascendance
Expands in all directions
As does this horizon
As morning's first light dawns upon you.

Tomorrow

Can be a tomorrow
If you let there be one
Just take a deep breath
As the density,
Begins to dissipate
You have endured
A tragic occurrence
Let peace and love,
Do what they're meant to
As you will go through
Stages in this crisis
Slowly, not all at once.
What you're experiencing
So happens when
You suffer such a loss
Hits harder than,
Anything ever has
Don't know which way to turn
But you receive support
From all who care.
Take time to heal
This leaves a void
Which will never be filled
But you will adapt.
In moments like this
You question your beliefs
About all that's come before
This is normal.

You are apt to change
To evolve your perspective
This causes a metamorphosis
In your way of thinking.
We all deal with grief
Individually
No two exactly the same
The nature of who are.
Life does go on
Can alter the rhythm
To a transcended version
In either one the sun will shine again.

Vibrant Center

Over my life times
Which are numerous
I have been on many worlds
In galaxies that stretch,
From one end to the other
In our universe
As I'm a traveller
In search of harmony.
There is continuity
I know western philosophy
Has a fear of death
But there's no dropping,
Off the edge of a cliff
Might be a short pause
Or an interlude
But no finality.
People will believe
What they want to
Or what they're told
Is the honest truth.
The trouble with this
Is that unless
You've touched a surface
The rest is hearsay.
I go beneath
To the root source
To be part of a wave
To flow in currents.
One learns the ways

Of the cycle they dwell in
While they're immersed
Within its elements.
You take on the image
From the residual effects
To blend as a rainbow
With all of your past striations.
If you were to peer inside
Your circles would reveal
These journeys bonded
To its vibrant center.

Days Of Old

To be happy
Is to be content
Knowing that here
At this moment,
The most precious time
Is sharing in a warmth
That surrounds us
As white flakes fall.
The air is frosty
Only adds to the atmosphere
A cherished closeness
As we remember,
The days of old
How it used to snow
The fun that we had
Playing endlessly.
So as it begins
These long, frigid nights
See us again
As we once were,
Laughing and frolicking
Being in the midst
Of those we dearly love
To rekindle these embers,
As ones who are able
Gather around
Talking, smiling
Even the odd tears of joy.
As we're fortunate

To be in the presence
Of our family
Who form a circle,
Some are missing
Who have passed on
Or could not make it
All are in our hearts and minds.
As we congregate
We do give thanks
For being near, not far
For seeing and holding our loved ones.

Binding Sinew

There is an opening
Along the wall of a mountain
Just feel for the breeze
You will know when,
Where you can enter
As you go inside
Will be quartz crystals
Drawing you to their zenith.
One in particular
Of your vibration
Will act as a beacon
Each belongs to the other.
This affinity
Has no boundaries
As you communicate
Across its membranes.
Similarities
Begin to reveal
A close connection
Upon all stratas.
Akin to a sibling
On one latitude
Two of one mind
Thoughts of equal measure.
You've had these ideas
But this serves its purpose
There is so much beyond
The limitations,
Of a physical existence

This is barely
Scratching the surface
Of what dwells beneath.
With this cognizance
Your vision expands
As do your wings
To touch upon,
With a dexterity
Wants not to disturb
But embrace in due course
That binding sinew.

Articulate Resonation

As you sit quietly
Your breathing slows
Nearly to the point
Of being soundless.
When you reach this rhythm
You are at a meter
That empowers
You to shift spheres.
Without even knowing
Solely by intention
So approach a lightness
Where you levitate.
No more upon the ground
But up in the air
In this ascension
You find serenity.
In this time and space
Time seems to stand still
In wave after wave
You roll with the tides.
So replenish
A rejuvenation
Don't look down upon
But across on an even keel.
Others like yourself
Have made this journey
Moments of self-reflection
In steps of realization.
From dimension to dimension

You see where you were
To where you are
In heights of elevation.
If anything
You're more of one mind
As thoughts once scattered
So gain a consensus.
They become intertwined
Like strands of perception
More closely defined
By an articulate resonation.

Lucid Leaf

The motion of a moment
Each like a heartbeat
Has its own particular
Specific resonation.
Look inside the movement
Find the true meaning
Listen intently
To its rhythm.
Hear the content
To the frequency
Of each breath of wind
As they correspond,
To poignant letters
String them together
As they bounce upon a breeze
To create a vision.
As you interpret
This spiritual mosaic
A path once ambiguous
Becomes coherent.
As you want to learn more
So do you sit in silence
In this meditative state
You are open,
To a higher knowledge
These keys are symbols
To which we gravitate
According to our cosmology.
The more you connect

The smoother is the transition
With these steps from
Their physical origins,
To the ascending esoteric
When you're in tune
Are akin to an instrument
Whose sounds have harmony.
As you flow along
Do so fluently
By a second nature
Now turns over its lucid leaf.

Then And There

You always meant to
Never found the time
To stop, look and see
At what frequently,
So caught your eye
Then came a day
You were free to roam
Decided then and there,
No more excuses
Curiosity was
Literally
Getting the better of you.
So in one went
Not knowing what
Would come of this
Only that it had to be.
The closer in proximity
These bells and whistles
Were sounding off
Deep within your recesses.
When at the gate
It was like as if
You had lost your breath
When it was only,
The beauty you were
Then beholding
As it was captivating
Almost intoxicating.
As you went inside

Knew you were in
The presence of
A magical aura.
Which was hovering
Then surrounding
For this was a destiny
That had waited its turn.
As your hands were immersed
You felt like the droplets
In a waterfall
When complete, you were transformed.

State Of Existence

Don't want to live a lie
Want to know the truth
We are not availed
Anything close,
To the real mark
Oh they so say
Society can't handle
What their select few know.
The only problem
They use this to
Their advantage
To control the masses.
There have been leaks
Of information
Which point towards
A re-balancing of sentience.
As people who re-incarnate
Come back with what
Is prior knowledge
That is way beyond,
What has ever been shared
These ideas are
Not radical
But a breath of fresh air.
Being kept away from
What is our destiny
Is a manipulation
To the highest degree.
People are not ignorant

They can reason enigmas out
Answers forthcoming
Shed a different light.
One that elucidates
Shows the state of existence
Not as they would have it
But the actual condition.
Which is far from the former
As the aperture opens
There is a release
Upon a plane of fertile minds.

Always Were

Those who we remember
In our blood line
Each and every day
In the calendar year.
Ones to be honoured
In their memory
Still vivid in our thoughts
Yet deep in our hearts.
Yes they have passed
From body to spirit
Not far from our eyes
For ones who believe,
An invisible pathway
With no doors in between
Connected by a bond
Eternal in its composition.
As in this length
We communicate
Back and forth along
By a telepathy.
The energy flow
In its abundant stream
Is in itself a constant
An infinite pool,
From which to draw upon
That buoys all involved
Within an orbit
Of endearment.
As long as they stay active

So do they remain
In sight, in touch
In integrated,
Not separate dimensions
To feel their presence
To be comforted
To share moments,
When even transformed
As here there are no walls
Only our imperfect selves
To be as we always were.

Voyage Of Compassion

You always have
Nice things to say
You had a good mom
That is for sure,
You open doors
So take the time
Go out of your way
To bring a smile,
To someone's face
Such is remarkable
In this day and age
Are above and beyond.
It's great to see
One of a kind
Sort of throwback
From an earlier period.
A quality
Is second to none
Heart on your sleeve
A genuine soul.
Like usual
You duck and hide
If you receive
An accolade.
What you think is nothing
Is the thought that counts
To be on your giving end
This means the world.
As it's not every day

Hardly at all
That one such as you
Is out there doing good deeds.
When this happens
It renews a faith
There is still out there
Those with a moral fiber.
The path you are on
An altruistic nature
Is by its own volition
A voyage of compassion.

Moment Of Silence

A moment of silence
For those who have fallen
Who've paid the price
With the ultimate sacrifice.
For their country
Whose voices are yet heard
As long as we remember
To know why we are here,
Able to move about
With our freedoms
These lives of meaning
Who served to protect.
Who did not die in vain
To stand against tyranny
With honour and integrity
With purposeful intent.
To still to this day
These spirits wish
To know why humans
Have not learned from the past.
That hatred and violence
Even now persist
To have to repeat
A dark legacy.
As long as there are
Those who exist
Who would put us asunder
Who revoke rights of others.
Hence, this is the reason

Why we can't turn our backs
But stand bravely
In the face of injustice.
As frustrating as it is
We can't capitulate
But fight as those
Before us did.
In ways to preserve
A dignity
To ensure that tomorrow
Is free of binding chains.

www.ingramcontent.com/pod-product-compliance
Lightning Source LLC
LaVergne TN
LVHW091049150826
845673LV00002B/516